PHOTO CHICAGO

PHOTO CHICAGO

BROWNTROUT PUBLISHERS
SAN FRANCISCO

PHOTO CHICAGO —a new way of looking at the great American city.

ARISING from the ashes of a devastating fire in 1871 Chicago was willed into being by the hard work and indomitable spirit of her citizens. Then as now those people came from around the world to the heart of America where the prairies and plains meet the Great Lakes. By applying new technology and civic daring to the building of their midwest metropolis Chicago became the quintessential American city.

Architecture and photography come together in this unique look at Chicago. No other American city can claim such wonders of the builders' trade as does Chicago. The broad prairies were like a blank canvas for Louis Sullivan, Frank Lloyd Wright, Mies van der Rohe and the other great architects to create their most fantastic designs. No mere photograph can convey the sense of space and form of a great building. But it can present the viewer the almost mystical beauty of wall, spire, and doorway.

This spectacular view was shot from the Sears Tower which was completed in 1974 and is the tallest building in the world. In the distance can be seen the John Hancock building on North Michigan Avenue.
Robert Holmes

The recently restored Buckingham Fountain in Grant Park across from
Congress Plaza was dedicated in 1927 by Kate Sturges Buckingham
in memory of her brother Clarence. It is based on a design found at
Versailles. *Jake Rajs*

This photo montage
of office buildings in the
'Loop' aptly represents
the dynamism of Chicago.
The financial and business
center of the midwest is
an everchanging panoply
of old and new.
Michael Townsend

Sitting behind the John G. Shedd Aquarium these visitors enjoy a beautiful scene: Lake Michigan in summer with the tall buildings of the Loop lining Lakeshore Drive. *Farrell Grehan*

13

This scene along the Chicago River is part of what many consider to be the most charming urban setting in America. *Farrell Grehan*

Many mid-summer visitors to Grant Park wish that they could join the figure in the fountain for a cool shower! *Farrell Grehan*

Fireworks explode over the north pier which in recent years has been converted into a shopping and tourist center. *Robert Holmes*

In 1967 one of the most controversial visitors ever to hit the Windy City was installed at the Daley Center. "The Picasso" may be a woman or it may be a cow—who knows? *Robert Holmes*

Wrigley Field remains the country's most revered baseball venue. Located off North Clark Street and opened in 1903, the home of the beloved Cubs still features many afternoon games. *Robert Holmes*

The glassy cold of winter can make the city's skyline shine as in this shot of Lake Michigan and Lakeshore Drive. *J. Wentworth*

At night the city's lights stretching off into the distance remind the visitor
that Chicago is the capitol of the Prairie. *Jake Rajs*

This inspiring photo of the Wrigley Building shows off the neo-Gothic
(sometimes referred to as "Woolworth Gothic") monument at its best.
Raymond's Hood's design won the $100,000 prize in 1922 and long
dominated the upper Loop. *Terry Donnelly*

Old Town is one of Chicago's many neighborhoods and includes won-
derful Victorian style houses and many interesting shops and businesses
such as the Old Town School of Folk Music. *Robert Holmes*

Here is portrayed the interior of the Chicago Library and Cultural Center
on Randolph Street and Michigan Avenue. *Robert Holmes*

The Art Institute of Chicago graces Michigan Avenue. In addition to the world-class museum the Institute is also an important training center for artists. *Michael Townsend*

29

The University of Chicago in Hyde Park on the South Side was
endowed in 1891 by John D. Rockefeller and has long been one
of the nation's most prestigious universities. *Robert Holmes*

The U of C's Rockefeller Chapel is a beautiful example of the Gothic architecture which typifies the campus. *C. & S. Chattopadhyay*

America's most celebrated architect, Frank Lloyd Wright, trained with Louis Sullivan and was a member of the Prairie School. His studio in Oak Park is shown here. *Robert Holmes*

Chicago was founded as Fort Dearborn in 1803. Looking at this photograph it is difficult to believe that barely two hundred years ago this great city was a wilderness. *Robert Holmes*

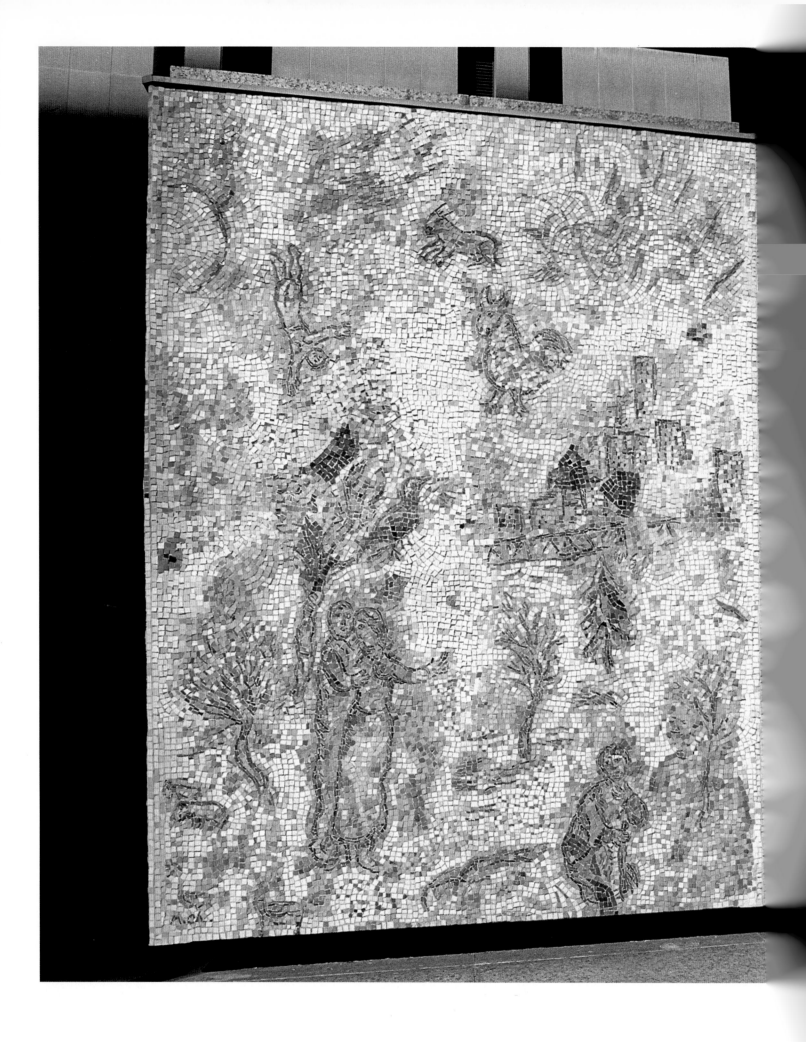

"The Four Seasons" mosaic by Marc Chagall graces the northeast end
of the First National Bank Plaza and was installed by the great artist in
1974. *Robert Holmes*

The Green Church is located in the Pullman Historic District on the far South Side. *Michael Townsend*

West of the Wrigley Building on the river are the twin towers of Bertrand Goldberg's Marina City, two of the most distinctive architectural designs in the city. *Robert Holmes*

Here the printing facility of the Chicago Sun-Times reminds us that
Chicago has always been a great newspaper town from the days of
The Front Page to the contemporary writing of Studs Terkel and
Mike Royko. *Robert Holmes*

The new Comiskey Park on the South Side is home to the
Chicago White Sox and is a symbol of the area's rejuvenation.
Michael Townsend

The Museum of Science and Industry was originally built to house
Fine Arts for the Columbian Exposition of 1893. It is located on South
Lakeshore Drive. *Robert Holmes*

Here is another view from behind the Shedd Aquarium in mid-summer.
Michael Townsend

Oak Street has become a popular shopping area on the North Side. Warm summer nights are perfect for the Promenade. *Robert Holmes*

Michigan Avenue has always been home to the finest shops which cater to visitors and locals alike. *Robert Holmes*

CHICAGO
PLACE

• SAKS FIFTH AVENUE •

The city has long been identified with the railroads which helped make
Chicago the transportation and meat-processing center of the country.

Robert Holmes

St. Patrick's Church is a visible reminder of Chicago's large and
politically powerful Irish community. *Robert Holmes*

This aerial photograph shows Chicago in early morning light. We are looking north along Lake Michigan. *Fred Hirschmann*

The Chicago River has been greatly cleaned up in the last twenty-five years so that it is now an important recreational resource. *Michael Townsend*

This interior view of the State of Illinois Building brings to mind the tension that has plagued relations between the great city/state of Chicago and rural downstate Illinois. *Michael Townsend*

Another view from the Sears Tower reveals the rich architectural mix of
Chicago. *Robert Holmes*

This statue of Nathan Hale guards the entrance to the Tribune
Building. The 'Trib' is another of Chicago's outstanding newspapers.
Robert Holmes

Here we have two views of Marshall Field's famous department store on State and Randolph streets. The founder's credo still stands: "Give the lady what she wants!" *Michael Townsend & Robert Holmes*

A misty aerial view from above Lincoln Park lets us remember that Chicago is on a large body of water and that the lake sometimes acts as inland sea with its own tides, fog, and 'effects'. *Fred Hirschmann*

The eighty stories of the Amoco Building tower above the Prudential Building which was the city's tallest building until the construction of the John Hancock Building in 1969. *Farrell Grehan*

The John Hancock Building has dominated the skyline of North Michigan Avenue since it was completed in 1969 making it the tallest building in the world up to that time. *Robert Holmes*

The ornate building that houses Carson Pirie Scott, a Chicago landmark department store, was designed by Louis Sullivan of Chicago's famous "Prairie School" of architecture. *Robert Holmes*

On the far South Side is the planned community of Pullman which was built to house the employees of the Palace Car Company. Pictured is the Florence House. *Robert Holmes*

Built in 1930 the massive Merchandise Mart contains more square feet than any other building in the country besides the Pentagon. *Robert Holmes*

Two classic symbols of Chicago—a blues saxophonist silhouetted in
front of the Water Tower, one of the few structures to survive the fire of
1871. *Robert Holmes*

Chicago has more parks per capita than any other major American city. Lincoln Park shown here has many attractions including a zoo, Shakespeare Garden, and the Lincoln Park Conservatory. *Robert Holmes*

The illuminated tower of the Tribune Building, built in 1922, is an apt symbol of the ambition of the paper's publisher, Colonel Robert McCormick. *Robert Holmes*

This interior of the Marquette Building, which was built in 1894, shows off the bas relief sculptures and murals that depict the city's history. *Robert Holmes*

Late night on Division Street is a time when the city is alive, the music is loud, and the politicians are all safely in bed! *Robert Holmes*

Chicago has over twenty miles of lakefront including some beautiful sandy beaches. *Farrell Grehan*

The Field Museum on Lakeshore Drive is one of the world's greatest
natural history museums and features exhibits as diverse as a Pawnee
earth lodge to the Mastaba tomb complex from ancient Egypt.

Michael Townsend

Here is another aerial view of the piers and Loop along Chicago's Lake
Michigan shoreline. *Fred Hirschmann*

The Adler Planetarium is another source of civic pride to Chicagoans and a great place to spend a hot summer afternoon. *Robert Holmes*

The Water Tower was built to house a thirty-seven foot pipe which was
used to equalize pressure with the Pumping Station across the street.
The building now houses the Chicago Visitors Center. *Farrell Grehan*

This view of West Wacker Drive shows the CTA (Chicago Transit Authority) elevated train entering the Loop. *Michael Townsend*

Chicago's ethnic mix has been a source of great pride, not to mention great food, since the city's founding. *Robert Holmes*

Chicago is truly the city of outdoor art. Here is pictured a piece by Joan Miro which graces the entrance to the Brunswick Building. *Michael Townsend*

The best way to see Chicago is on foot—but watch out for the cars on North Michigan Avenue! *Michael Townsend*